Families

Foster Parents

Revised Edition

Rebecca Rissman

Heinemann Library
Chicago, Illinois

www.capstonepub.com
Visit our website to find out more information about Heinemann-Raintree books.

To order:

Phone 800-747-4992
Visit www.capstonepub.com to browse our catalog and order online.

© 2011, 2021 Heinemann Library
an imprint of Capstone Global Library, LLC
Chicago, Illinois

All rights reserved. No part of this publication may be reproduced or transmitted in any form or by any means, electronic or mechanical, including photocopying, recording, taping, or any information storage and retrieval system, without permission in writing from the publisher.

Edited by Rebecca Rissman and Catherine Veitch
Designed by Ryan Frieson
Picture research by Tracy Cummins
Originated by Capstone Global Library Ltd

Library of Congress Cataloging-in-Publication Data is available on the Library of Congress website.
ISBN 9781484668313 (pb)

Acknowledgments
We would like to thank the following for permission to reproduce photographs: Getty Images: 10'000 Hours, 11, 12, Camille Tokerud, 21, Cavan Images, cover, Ed Bock, 18, Fuse, 15, Hill Street Studios, 14, Jeremy Woodhouse, 22, Kevin Dodge, 8, Mayur Kakade, 6, Tom Stoddart Archive, 5; iStockphoto: Alexander Shalamov, 9, paldomurillo, 20; Shutterstock: BlueOrange Studio, back cover, 13, 23, DNF Style, 17, 23, Golden Pixels LLC, 16, Juice Dash, 4, LightField Studios, 7, Monkey Business Images, 10, 23, Tomasz Markowski, 19

We would like to thank Anne Pezalla and Nancy Harris for their invaluable help in the preparation of this book.

Every effort has been made to contact copyright holders of any material reproduced in this book. Any omissions will be rectified in subsequent printings if notice is given to the publisher.

Printed in the United States 6012

Contents

What Is a Family? 4

What Are Families Like? 8

What Is Foster Care? 10

Who Are Foster Parents? 12

Children Living with Foster Parents 18

Do You Know? 22

Picture Glossary. 23

Index 24

What Is a Family?

A family is a group of people. People in families are called family members.

The people in families care for each other.

All families are different.

All families are special.

What Are Families Like?

Some families are big.

Some families are small.

What Is Foster Care?

Foster care makes sure children are cared for.

Foster care puts children with new families.

Who Are Foster Parents?

Foster children's new parents are called foster parents.

Foster parents care for the children.

Some foster parents care for children for a long time.

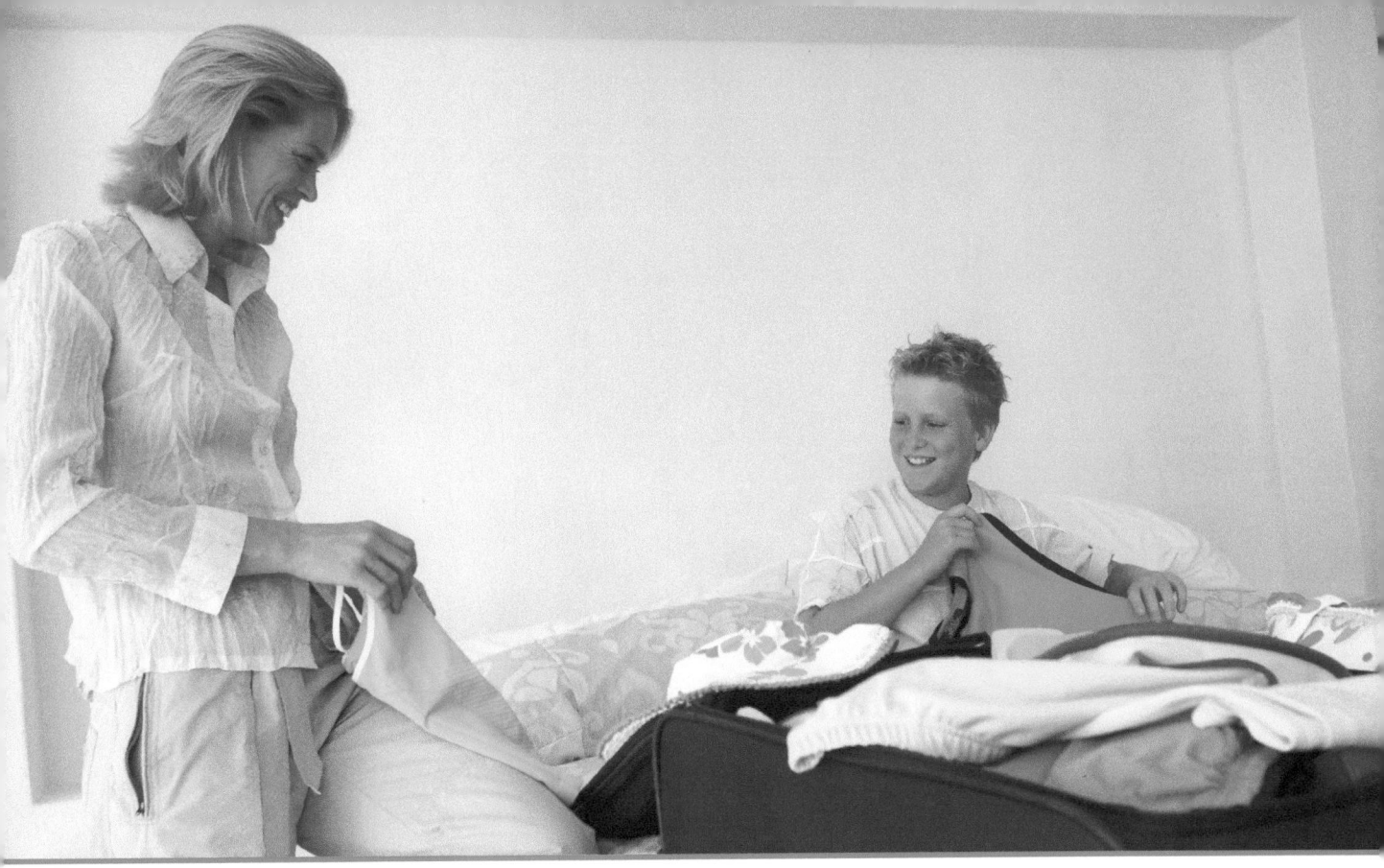

Some foster parents care for children for a short time.

Some foster parents care for one child.

Some foster parents care for more than one child.

Children Living with Foster Parents

Some foster parents care for children who have been hurt.

Foster parents care for children whose parents could not care for them.

Some children leave their foster parents to live with their parents again.

Some children leave their foster parents to live with new families.

Do You Know?

Do you know any foster parents?

Picture Glossary

foster care helps keep children safe and cared for

foster parent adult who looks after children that are not their own

member person who belongs to a group

Index

family members 4
foster care 10, 11
foster parent 12, 13, 14, 15, 16 17, 18, 19, 20, 21, 22

Note to Parents and Teachers

Before Reading

Explain to children that foster care is a special system that makes sure all children are cared for and safe. Some children are in foster care for a short time, and then return to their families. Other children are in foster care until they can be adopted by new families. Explain that adoption is a system that places children with new families.

After Reading

Discuss with children how foster parents help children in need. Some children in foster care require special attention that their parents may not have been able to give to them. Other children in foster care were not able to live with their parents because they were unsafe.

© 2008, 2016 Heinemann Library
a division of Capstone Global Library, LLC.
Chicago, Illinois

To contact Capstone Global Library please call 800-747-4992 or visit our website www.mycapstone.com

All rights reserved. No part of this publication may be reproduced or transmitted in any form or by any means, electronic or mechanical, including photocopying, recording, taping, or any information storage and retrieval system, without permission in writing from the publisher.

Picture research: Erica Martin, Hannah Taylor and Ginny Stroud-Lewis
Designed by Philippa Jenkins

Library of Congress Cataloging-in-Publication Data
Guillain, Charlotte.
Reusing and recycling revised edition / Charlotte Guillain.
p. cm. -- (Help the environment)
Includes bibliographical references and index.
ISBN-13: 978-1-4329-0888-1 (hc)
ISBN-13: 978-1-4846-3566-7 (pb)
ISBN-13: 978-1-4846-0081-8 (Saddle Stitch)
1. Recycling (Waste, etc.)--Juvenile literature. I. Title.
TD792.G85 2008
363.72'82--dc22
2007041173

Acknowledgments
The author and publisher would like to thank the following for permission to reproduce photographs: Getty Images: Jupiterimages, 19; iStockphoto: fcafotodigital, 14, 20 (bottom left), SupharoekBK, 10; Capstone Studio: 6, 7, 8, 9, 20 (top left & top right), 23 (bottom); Shutterstock: blvdone, 4 (bottom left), Carlos Horta, 12, Evan Lorne, 17, Hurst Photo, back cover, 21, James R. Martin, 15, 23 (middle), Matej Kastelic, 22, Miks Mihails Ignats, 4 (top right), 23 (top), Monkey Business Images, 5, Rosomak, 4 (bottom right), RTimages, 13, 20 (bottom right), sunsetman, cover, szefei, 4 (top left), Teresa Kasprzycka, 11, Tyler Olson, 16, 18

Every effort has been made to contact copyright holders of any material reproduced in this book.
Any omissions will be rectified in subsequent printings if notice is given to the publishers.

Printed in the United States 4512